Giraffes

Lizzie Cope

Illustrated by Francesca Rosa

Additional illustrations by Gal Weizman

Giraffe consultant: Professor David Macdonald CBE,
Wildlife Conservation Research Unit, Zoology Department, University of Oxford
Reading consultant: Alison Kelly

Contents

Giraffes can live until they're over 25 years old.

Giraffes in Africa

There are nine different types of giraffes. They all live in Africa.

This mother giraffe and her babies are Angolan giraffes.

Towering high

Giraffes are the tallest animals in the world.

A giraffe has a very, very long neck.

Its legs are long and powerful.

Its hooves are as wide as big plates.

This giraffe has two hairy bumps on top of its head.

They're called ossicones.

There are only seven bones in a giraffe's neck. That's the same as you have in yours.

Lots of spots

Giraffes have very short fur with brown patches. Each type of giraffe has a different pattern of patches.

Reticulated giraffes have big patches with pale lines in between.

The patches on Kordofan giraffes are light brown.

Masai giraffes' patches are shaped like leaves.

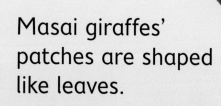

Giraffes' patches blend in with trees. This helps them to hide and keep safe.

Living together

Giraffes live in groups called herds. There can be as many as 50 of them in a herd.

This herd is crossing a grassy plain, called a savannah.

Savannahs are hot and often very dry. They're dotted with trees.

If the giraffes come to a river, they walk through the water.

When it gets too hot, they rest in the shade.

Sometimes herds of giraffes and zebras walk across savannahs together.

Eating plants

Giraffes eat different parts of bushes and trees, but mostly they eat leaves.

This giraffe is stretching up to reach the leaves.

Giraffes also bend down to eat leaves near the ground.

They eat twigs and flowers too...

...and sometimes they eat fruit.

Giraffes eat mud because it contains salt. They need salt to stay healthy.

Tongue tricks

Every giraffe has a very long tongue that it can bend. It's good for picking leaves.

A giraffe wraps its tongue around the branch of a tree.

Then it rips off the leaves and pulls them into its mouth.

Giraffes' tongues have thick skin to protect them from sharp thorns.

Giraffes' tongues can be purple, dark blue or black.

A giraffe also uses its tongue to wash its face.

See how this giraffe is licking its nose clean.

Drinking up

Every few days, giraffes search for rivers and watering holes so they can drink.

A thirsty giraffe stands with its front legs wide apart.

Then it bends down to suck some water into its mouth.

As it lifts its head, the water flows down to its tummy.

When it's very hot, watering holes dry up.

This Angolan giraffe has found some water to drink.

Giraffes get most of the water they need from the plants they eat.

Bull giraffes

Male giraffes are called bulls. They're taller and heavier than female giraffes.

Bull giraffes often live together in small herds.

Sometimes one of the bulls leaves to live on his own.

Later, the bull searches for female giraffes to have babies with them.

Bull giraffes fight to see who is strongest.

These bulls are trying to slam their necks into each other.

Big babies

A mother giraffe carries her baby inside her for about 15 months. A baby giraffe is called a calf.

When a calf is born, it falls to the ground. The calf isn't hurt.

Then the calf rests while its mother gently licks it clean.

After just one hour, the calf stands up and starts to walk.

This mother
is nuzzling her
young calf, so
they get used to
each other's smell.

Growing up

Giraffe calves grow up quickly.

This calf is drinking its mother's milk. The milk helps it to grow strong.

When it's only one day old, a calf can already run quickly.

After a few weeks, the mother takes her calf to meet the herd.

She also shows it which types of plants it can eat.

These young giraffes are from the same herd. They're playing together.

Annoying insects

Giraffes try to keep insects off their bodies.

They swing their tails from side to side to flick away flies.

Their long eyelashes protect their eyes when they blink.

They sometimes rub against branches to scratch itchy insect bites.

The birds on this giraffe are called oxpeckers.

They're eating insects in its fur.

Giraffe noises

Giraffes only make a few sounds.
They're very quiet most of the time.

But at night they sometimes
make low humming noises.

Nobody knows why giraffes do this.

When a giraffe spots a dangerous animal,
it snorts to warn its herd.

A young giraffe makes mooing sounds to
call for its mother.

Look out!

Giraffes keep watch for lions, leopards and hyenas that try to hunt them.

A giraffe spots a lion hiding in some long grass.

At first, it tries to scare off the lion by staring at it.

Then it kicks with its hooves until the lion goes away.

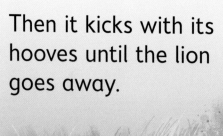

Giraffes can run very fast if they need to escape.

These two are sprinting across the hot, dry savannah.

Light sleepers

Giraffes don't need much sleep. They just have short naps during the day and night.

This sleepy giraffe is resting its head on its back leg.

Giraffes can stay standing up while they sleep.

When giraffes sleep, they sometimes keep their eyes half open.

Calves often rest together. An adult from their herd watches over them.

Glossary

Here are some of the words in this book you might not know. This page tells you what they mean.

 hoof - the hard part at the end of a giraffe's foot.

 ossicone - a bump on a giraffe's head. Some ossicones are very furry.

 herd - a large or small group of giraffes who live together.

 savannah - a grassy plain with very few trees and bushes.

 watering hole - a pool of water where animals drink.

 bull - a male giraffe. Adult bulls often live on their own or in small herds.

 calf - a baby giraffe. Most mother giraffes have one calf at a time.

Usborne Quicklinks

Would you like to find out more about giraffes, and watch them run across the savannah? Visit Usborne Quicklinks for links to websites with videos, facts and activities.

Go to **usborne.com/Quicklinks** and type in the keywords "**beginners giraffes**". Make sure you ask a grown-up before going online.

Notes for grown-ups

Please read the internet safety guidelines at Usborne Quicklinks with your child. Children should be supervised online. The websites are regularly reviewed and the links at Usborne Quicklinks are updated. However, Usborne Publishing is not responsible and does not accept liability for the content or availability of any website other than its own.

These giraffes are rubbing their noses together to say hello.

Index

Acknowledgements

Designed by Sam Whibley, Jenny Hastings and Claire Morgan
Photographic manipulation by John Russell and Nick Wakeford

Photo credits
The publishers are grateful to the following for permission to reproduce material:
cover © Ben Denison/500px/Getty Images; **p.1** © Mario Moreno/Getty Images; **pp.2-3** © Philippe-Alexandre Chevallier/Biosphoto/SuperStock; **p.4** © Bill Gozansky/Alamy Stock Photo; **p.5** © Leonhard Leichtle/500px/Getty Images; **p.7** © Oleg Breslavtsev/Alamy Stock Photo; **pp.8-9** © Richard Garvey-Williams/Alamy Stock Photo; **p.10** © Denis-Huot/naturepl.com; **p.12** © James Hager/Getty Images; **p.13** © Jane Rix/Alamy Stock Photo; **p.15** © Bill Gozansky/age fotostock/SuperStock; **p.17** © Michel & Christine Denis-Huot/Biosphoto/SuperStock; **p.19** © Mary McDonald/naturepl.com; **p.20** © Ibrahim Suha Derbent/Getty Images; **p.21** © Yva Momatiuk & John Eastcott/Minden Pictures/Alamy Stock Photo; **p.21** © William Warby/Creative commons; **p.22** © Christopher Wedd/Alamy Stock Photo; **p.23** © Uwe Skrzypczak/imageBROKER/Alamy Stock Photo; **p.24** © Peter Blackwell/naturepl.com; **p.27** © Claude Huot/Alamy Stock Photo; **p.28** © D. M. Sheldon/Tierfotoagentur/Alamy Stock Photo; **p.31** © Li Jia/Getty Images.

Sun, Moon and Stars

Farm Animals

Elizabeth I

Rubbish & Recycling

Dogs

Horses and ponies

Spiders

Planes

Cats

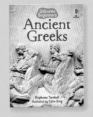
Ancient Greeks

Volcanoes

Dinosaurs

Your Body

Armour

Sharks

The Celts

Vikings

Castles

How flowers grow

Digging up the past

Caterpillars & Butterflies

Ballet

Pirates

Egyptians

Eggs & Chicks

Romans

Weather

Tadpoles & Frogs

Why do we eat?

Under the Sea

Bears

AZTECS

Trucks

Night Animals

Firefighters

Antarctica

Bugs

COWBOYS

PLANET EARTH

London

Seashore

China

Dangerous Animals

Rainforests

Trees

Reptiles

Ships

Bats

Trains

The Solar System

Knights

Monkeys

Penguins

Elephants

Tigers

Earthquakes & Tsunamis

Storms and Hurricanes

BEES & WASPS

Wolves

Owls